Preface

This exhibition brings to the Barber Institute a superb selection of nineteenth-century Swedish landscape paintings, ranging from Romantic depictions of vast open spaces to Realist and Symbolist responses to nature. Scandinavian art is little known in Britain, and this is a unique opportunity for the public to familiarise themselves with the powerful achievements of specifically Swedish landscapists. It is not the first time that we have showcased Nordic landscape, however, and the exhibition builds on the success of *Moonrise over Europe: J C Dahl and Romantic Landscape*, which was mounted here in 2006 and contextualised our picture, *Mother and Child by the Sea*, a moonlit masterpiece by Dahl, the leading Norwegian landscapist of the 19th century.

The exhibition is a collaboration with the Nationalmuseum, Stockholm, and has been curated by our Senior Curator, Paul Spencer-Longhurst, who has written an excellent introduction to the development of Swedish landscape between about 1850 and 1910. He has worked closely with the Swedish curators, Mikael Ahlund and Per Hedström, who gave much time and thought to the selection of the works and their interpretation for a British audience. While some of the artists may be known here, such as Marcus Larson, others, like Gustav Rydberg, Elias Erdtman and Otto Hesselbom will be entirely new - and visitors may be surprised to see a painting by August Strindberg, more familiar as a dramatist and novelist.

It has been a pleasure to work with our colleagues in Stockholm at a time when they are mounting the first major exhibition of Pre-Raphaelite paintings in Sweden, to which we are lending *The Blue Bower* by Dante Gabriel Rossetti. My thanks are extended to them and to our Friends' organisation for their generous support, as well as all the staff at the Barber Institute for their dedication and hard work in bringing together this exhibition, which I am sure will be a triumph for both institutions.

Ann Sumner,
Director.

Acknowledgements

Many people have contributed to the preparation of this exhibition and catalogue. To all of them I am most grateful, and among them I would like to acknowledge with special appreciation the co-operation, assistance and enthusiasm of Louise Adkin, Mikael Ahlund, Karin Altenberg, John van Boolen, Andy Bott, Sarah Brown, H.E. Staffan Carlsson, Hugh Carslake, Liane and Maurizio Crisari, Andrew Davies, Torsten Gunnarsson, David Gwyther, Per Hedström, Yvonne Locke, Maxyne McDonald, Kathryn Murray, Peter Owen, Karen Parker, Rosemary Poynton, Lionel Quigley, Christopher Riopelle, Brian Scholes, Ann Sumner, Joanne Sweet, Sir David Wilson and Sophie Wilson. I am much beholden to the Trustees of the Barber Institute for their moral and financial backing, and to my curatorial and academic colleagues for their generous forbearance over my recent unavailability for other duties. As ever I owe a great debt of gratitude to Sue, Rose and Flora Spencer-Longhurst for unstinting support, encouragement and, from time to time, consolation.

To the sole lender, the Nationalmuseum Stockholm, we are deeply indebted. Not only have our colleagues there allowed 29 prime examples of Swedish landscape a three-month leave of absence from their own definitive displays, but they have also permitted us to benefit from generous concessions to their standard terms of loan, as well as providing enthusiastic and much appreciated co-operation in the compilation of this catalogue.

The Friends of the Barber Institute have been particularly generous in financing the catalogue, which we hope will stand as a worthy record, not only of the exhibition, but also of their warm support of the Institute and its projects over the years. To them we are once more extremely grateful.

Paul Spencer-Longhurst,
Senior Curator.

northernlights

Swedish Landscapes from the Nationalmuseum, Stockholm

Paul Spencer-Longhurst

The Barber Institute of Fine Arts - University of Birmingham
27 February - 31 May 2009

Contents

'The History of Natural Beauty'
Swedish Landscape Painting 1850 - 1910

In the 19th century, Sweden was perceived in much of western Europe as vast, remote and empty. Even as late as 1900 it had a population of only a few million as compared with the 35 million of Britain, a land one third of its size. The inhabitants were dispersed over vast areas, industrialisation arrived late and travel was difficult - there was little railway construction, for example, before 1860. For over two hundred years, Sweden had been the dominant power in Scandinavia but in the Napoleonic upheaval of Europe she lost Finland to Russia in 1809, gaining Norway five years later, which remained part of her territory until 1905. During this period Sweden's artistic development was slow and hesitant. For the first half of the century, advances in Scandinavian painting took place mainly elsewhere - in Norway with the pioneering landscapist, Johan Christian Dahl (1788-1857) and in Denmark with its 'golden age' of classical landscape and naturalistic genre painting, headed by Christoffer Wilhelm Eckersberg (1783-1853), Constantin Hansen (1804-80), Christen Købke (1810-48) and their contemporaries.

By contrast, Swedish painting was heterogeneous in style. Cultural affinity with nature, often attributed to the variety and rigours of the Swedish climate, was overlaid with an ideal of landscape stemming partly from the classical tradition but deriving also from the northern forest landscapes, rocky mountainous scenes and waterfalls of the Dutch seventeenth-century artists, Allart van Everdingen and Jacob van Ruisdael. These decades were also characterised by Romantic tendencies, frequently imported from Germany.

Images of Old Norse culture were common to Scandinavian artists but gained currency in Sweden after the loss of Finland, when myths and wilderness themes came to play a significant role as symbols of national integrity, strength and vigour. The barren and desolate were redefined and their intrinsic value recast, with clear moral overtones. Simultaneously many Swedes, notably Gustav Wilhelm Palm, made their way to Rome, which until about 1850 was an artistic mecca for Scandinavian painters (cats. 20 & 21). Few, however, devoted themselves to classical landscape after their return. Conversely, Carl Johan Fahlcrantz neither went to Italy nor saw any painting by the seventeenth century progenitor of classical landscape, Claude Lorrain, and few, if any, by his Dutch followers, yet produced perfect reprises of his work (cat. 19), even though they must have been based solely on his knowledge of prints, such as Richard Earlom's popular engraved *Liber Veritatis*, first published in 1777.

However, by 1850 Swedish art was beginning to develop distinctive characteristics, inspired initially by impulses from abroad. That year, a great Nordic art exhibition was held in Stockholm which established the north German city of Düsseldorf as the new artistic centre for the Swedes, rather than Rome and confirmed the increasing importance of Romantic landscape and idealised genre painting as subject matter. In 1839 a chair in landscape had been established at the Academy there and from 1854 to 1862 this was held by the Norwegian fjord-painter, Hans Gude (1825-1903). Young artists were attracted to the city in considerable numbers, culminating around 1860, when seventy Swedes were studying there.

Some began to find a solution to the problem of creating a national artistic identity for their country in the teaching of Gude and his fellow Norwegian, Adolph Tidemand (1814-76). Among them, Marcus Larson learned to place much emphasis on mood in his pictures, leading to a tendency towards the sublime or heroic, later developed into a taste for wild and untouched nature (cats. 2 & 22). In the works of other Swedish artists, too, the sublimities of the wilderness were becoming recognised as a quintessential element of Swedish cultural and political identity. In 1853, when the Crown Prince (later King Charles XV), himself an artist, was made Chancellor of the Stockholm Academy of Art, he encouraged patriotic landscape with the following words: 'We have a wonderful country, perhaps not radiant in sunshine but all the more in seriousness and vigour. Our history and traditions are rich and poetic, full of noble memories, which with good reason constitute our honours and our pride. And so the

M. Larson, *Norwegian Fjord in Moonlight* (cat. 2, detail)

history of natural beauty of this, the land of our fathers, shall be the main subject of our art - together they build a temple, and thus shall the work of our artists be also the worship of our Lord of nature, the Almighty God.' [1]

Twenty years later, France became the artistic capital for aspiring Swedish artists in search of less artificial subject matter. Realism came late to Sweden as a style, emerging from tentative beginnings such as Gustav Rydberg's *Spring in Skåne* (cat. 3). The first Swede to adopt the rural landscape painting style of the Barbizon artists was Alfred Wahlberg (cat. 4), who in turn attracted the attention of Carl Fredrik Hill. In the mid-1870s it was Hill who developed a type of painting that, by virtue of its intensity and technical innovations, must be considered among the most pioneering of the period (cat. 6). Stockholm in the mid-1880s witnessed the formation of a group of young artists under the name of the 'Opponents' in opposition to the outmoded instruction of the Academy of Arts. In 1886 they went on to found the Artists' Association (*Konstnärsförbundet*), comprising leading radical painters of the day, many of whom had developed *plein-air* Realist styles while studying in France. A number of them, including Bruno Liljefors (cat. 10), Nils Kreuger (cat. 15), and Karl Nordström (cat. 29), had been part of an influential international artists' colony there in the small village of Grez-sur-Loing, south of Paris. This group was also visited by the prominent writer and critic August Strindberg, who during the 1870s produced some small pictures in Stockholm, and was a friend of many of the artists there, though he did not turn seriously to painting until the 1890s (cat. 12). Anders Zorn also pursued a French training, influenced principally by Manet and the Impressionists, in addition to his studies of the British watercolour tradition in London (cat. 27). Buoyant Realism was triumphant in the 1885 Opponents' Stockholm exhibition, and the following year Carl Larsson (1853-1919) exhibited his large and challenging picture, *The Open-Air Painter* (Nationalmuseum) at the Paris Salon, showing himself swathed in furs and doggedly painting in the freezing air of a snowbound Stockholm (fig. 1). It was well received, but by then themes and styles had moved on in Paris, where focal works at the Salon now included Whistler's wraithlike evocations and the etiolated allegories of Puvis de Chavannes. By the end of the 1880s, however, most Swedish artists had returned from France and the blond palette and tonal painting pioneered by the Impressionists began to be replaced by colours more suitable to climatic conditions in Sweden. About 1890 a strong surge in the Swedish economy revitalised artistic life,

Fig. 1 Carl Larsson, *The Open-Air Painter* (Nationalmuseum, Stockholm, detail)

leading to increased private patronage and the growth of independent centres outside Stockholm, particularly Gothenburg and Malmö. Painters looked to the Swedish countryside for their subject matter, often in hitherto ignored areas, and many, including Zorn, settled there permanently. The 1890s emerged as the decade of National Romanticism as they developed what was deemed to be a truly Swedish landscape repertoire - forests and lakes, remote provinces, regional characteristics, the icy magic of winter and haunting summer twilights. These subjects were increasingly couched in a style characterised by blurred spatial boundaries, neglect of perspective and a rejection of any fixed viewpoint in favour of simplified composition and monumental structure. Many artists devoted themselves to a type of mood landscape *(stämningsmåleri)*, overlaid with elements of Symbolism suggesting a correspondence between external forms and subjective states of mind. Noting the break with Realism, the artist Richard Bergh wrote in 1896, 'Instinctively the evocative painter seeks a light, a mood in nature, a clime beyond which he can locate a spirit possessing the torments and delights of his own soul, its dreams of light and dark.' [2] That landscape painting reached a zenith in Sweden during the 1890s was linked by Bergh to a national revolt against the ever-encroaching materialism of the decade and a gathering anxiety over its existential uncertainties. 'The tenuous spiritual moods of our century', he wrote, 'the indeterminate longing, the doubts and yearnings, the natural counterweight to the sober life that we otherwise lead, fenced in on all sides by science - have found in music and the art of landscape just that vague, intangible expression they need to become alive and perceptible to our consciousness.' [3]

This evocative landscape painting, expressed in a Symbolist idiom, with ample simplified forms, was undeniably susceptible to external influences, especially the decorative linearity and non-naturalistic colours of Gauguin and Van Gogh. Their paintings and the work of other Post-Impressionists were known to Swedish artists not only through individual journeys to France but especially through a major exhibition held in Copenhagen in 1893, where 29 pictures by Van Gogh were shown, together with 51 works by Gauguin, including ten straight from Tahiti. By the early 1900s the Expressionism of Munch and the sinuous fluencies of Art Nouveau were also having a major effect.

In the half-century under review, the main force driving Swedish landscapists remained the enormous impact of the vast and varied landscape itself. But their response was transformed from the derivative and academic by the original contributions of many, especially the novel working methods of C.F. Hill and

A. Zorn, *Study of Landscape from Mora* (cat. 27, detail)

August Strindberg followed by the almost transcendental visions of Eugène Jansson (cats. 6, 12 & 16). In the decades from 1880 to 1910 they explored, interpreted and celebrated what had once been deemed 'the land with nothing to paint' [4] on a scale and with a variety of meaning hitherto unknown, achieving a unique identity for themselves and for Swedish landscape painting.

Within its vibrant development at this time, their pictures stand out as beacons of originality and milestones in the formation and documentation of a quintessentially Swedish national consciousness. They hold their own not only within the general Scandinavian context, dominated by the proto-Expressionist visions of Munch or the figurative works of Zorn, but also in the international Post-Impressionist and Symbolist traditions deriving from Gauguin and Van Gogh. Late nineteenth-century Swedish landscape deserves much greater recognition outside its own country - a deficiency to which it is hoped that the present exhibition will be a significant corrective.

———————————●———————————

Notes

[1] Torsten Gunnarsson, *Nordic Landscape Painting in the Nineteenth Century*, translated by Nancy Adler, 1998, p. 115 & p. 276, n. 30. The present essay and following catalogue entries are heavily indebted to this publication, henceforth cited as 'Gunnarsson' and to other English-language publications by the same author.

[2] R. Bergh: *Karl Nordström och det Nordiska stämningslandskapet* [*Karl Nordström and the Evocative Nordic Landscape*], 1896; cited by Gunnarsson, p. 277, n. 1

[3] R. Bergh, *loc.cit.*, cited by Gunnarsson, p. 277, n. 2

[4] R. Bergh in 'Svenskt konstnärskynne', 1899 as representing the Opponent generation's view of the Swedish countryside; cited by Gunnarsson, p. 278, n. 33.

Catalogue

Paintings

1 **Carl Johan Fahlcrantz (1774-1861)**
A Waterfall, Älvkarleby
Oil on canvas, 49 x 67 cm.
Undated
Nationalmuseum NM 4768

The early years of the 19th century witnessed a growing interest in Romantic landscape painting in Sweden, which Fahlcrantz set out to satisfy with a style hovering between those of his seventeenth-century exemplars, Jacob van Ruisdael and Claude Lorrain (cf. cat. 19). From 1815 he was professor at the Academy, Stockholm, and with no major rivals as landscapists became the pre-eminent artist in Sweden until the end of the 1840s. Grounded in the art of Elias Martin (1739-1818), his works also have a spiritual affinity with the German Romantic tradition and those of his Norwegian contemporary, Johan Christian Dahl (1788-1857). Älvkarleby lies at the seaward end of the Hedesundafjord, on the east coast of Sweden, near Gävle on the Gulf of Bothnia off the Baltic Sea. The area is traditionally regarded as the climatic and cultural boundary to the north of the country as indicated by the prominent coniferous trees. Human presence is shown as small and insignificant, and the power of untamed nature is further underlined by the threatening sky and dramatic force of the River Dalälven, plunging down the falls and spreading out to fill the entire foreground.

2 **Marcus Larson (1825-1864)**
Norwegian Fjord in Moonlight: Motif from the Sogne-Fjord
Oil on canvas,130 x 177 cm.
Signed and dated 1861
Nationalmuseum NM 2000

On completing his studies at the Stockholm Academy, Larson produced marine paintings in collaboration with his student friend, Kilian Zoll, and during a stay in Düsseldorf he became increasingly interested in dramatic seascapes. In 1850 he was inspired by the Nordic Art Exhibition, held in Stockholm, to make a visit to Norway - a turning point in his career. There he produced studies of the Sogne-Fjord, on the west coast, north of Bergen, which were then incorporated into works such as this, inspired by the numerous nocturnal scenes of Fahlcrantz, where light creates the mood and holds the composition together in a coherent whole. He also painted shipwrecks and Swedish scenery in a style that was reminiscent of the dramatic mountain landscapes prevalent in Norwegian painting, especially in the work of J.C. Dahl and Thomas Fearnley (1802-42). Larson was particularly famous for his tempestuous Småland landscapes (cat. 22). Here, however, he exploits to the full the Romantic fascination with moonlight, used together with the glow of the man-made fire to intensify this haunting, sublime setting, redolent of Old Norse legend.

3 **Gustav Rydberg (1835-1933)**
Spring in Skåne
Oil on canvas, 46 x 64 cm.
Signed and dated 1868
Nationalmuseum NM 1059

Rydberg was one of the most faithful portrayers of Skåne, the southernmost province of Sweden. The present work is a major example of Swedish Realism, where an everyday subject has been represented in an unassertive range of browns, endowing it with its own value, and perhaps reflecting the lessons absorbed by the artist during his period spent in Copenhagen (1852-7), as well as the ideals of Alfred Wahlberg, with whom he often painted (cat. 4). Although the damp coldness of the scene is palpable, with barely any hint of spring, apart from the melting snow, this is a composed work, for the oak trees are known to have been derived from sketches made by the artist in the Stockholm area. Rydberg was particularly admired in his own day for his convincing representation of atmosphere and illusionist rendering of reflections in still water, as seen here beneath the cart. The painting was bought by the Nationalmuseum in the year of its execution - a fitting tribute to the opening of the new building two years earlier.

4   Alfred Wahlberg (1834-1906)

View near Vaxholm
Oil on canvas, 71 x 110 cm.
Signed and dated 1872
Nationalmuseum NM 1641

Wahlberg was one of the last Swedes to study under Hans Gude at the *Kunstakademie* in Düsseldorf, where he arrived in 1857. In the autumn of 1866, however, after four years in Sweden, he became the first to move to Paris, encouraged by King Charles XV and fired by an exhibition of Barbizon works, which he had seen at Brussels in 1860. In Paris he recognised the value of *plein-air* painting - a development reflected in this picture, suffused with a typically 'French' grey haze. He achieved recognition at the Salon as early as 1870 and for several years was one of the most admired foreign painters in Paris, returning to Sweden in the summers, where he greatly influenced the younger generation of artists, such as Wilhelm von Gegerfelt (1844-1920) and Carl Fredrik Hill (cat. 6). Together with those of Edvard Bergh (cats. 5 and 26) his landscapes came to mark the transition to Realism, as noted by Strindberg in 1879: 'Here all things are themselves … clearly and definitely drawn, distinctly modelled, each with their own colours we see them …'. The island of Vaxholm lies offshore from Stockholm, renowned for its fortress that once protected the waterways of the city.

Wachholm. 1872.   Wfr. Wahlberg

5   **Edvard Bergh (1828-1880)**
Summer Landscape
Oil on canvas, 60 x 90 cm.
Signed and dated 1873
Nationalmuseum NM 3084

Best known for his tranquil lake scenes, Bergh was a pupil of Hans Gude, Professor of Landscape at the Düsseldorf Academy. His early work focused on grandiose mountain and wilderness scenes in the manner of Fahlcrantz and Larson but by the 1870s he had progressed to the pasturelands, birch copses and sparkling lakes of middle Sweden. He took a long time to find an appropriate way of realistically conveying these undramatic locations but here, in a setting reminiscent of Aelbert Cuyp's seventeenth-century pastoral scenes, he brilliantly evokes the long, languorous summer days for which Sweden is renowned. Bergh was well received by the public, becoming the Stockholm Academy's first teacher of landscape painting in 1858. Ten years later he was given the newly established professorial chair in the subject. His work paved the way for the more radical paintings of the 'Paris Swedes' such as C.F. Hill and Axel Lindman (cats. 6, 7 & 8).

6   **Carl Fredrik Hill (1849-1911)**
      The Beach at Luc
      Oil on canvas, 46.5 x 61.5 cm.
      Signed; 1876
      Nationalmuseum NM 6065

Hill was the most innovative Swedish and indeed Scandinavian landscapist of the 1870s. His works possess a powerful emotional charge yet his great creative period in France lasted only for the four years to 1877. After moving to Paris in 1873, he travelled between a number of small communities in that region and on the Normandy coast, including Montigny, near Grez-sur-Loing, and Luc-sur-Mer, a small fishing village and bathing resort north of Caen. Attracted by its long beaches and steep cliffs, he stayed for a month in August 1876, producing 17 canvases. The innovative technique of this picture, involving the use of a palette knife and pieces of glass, recalls the powerful brushwork and vibrant impasto of French Realists such as Courbet and the ideas of the Impressionists about the appropriate distance at which to view a work. Its very emptiness was challenging to the contemporary eye and its uncomposed aspect suggests that it was painted from nature. Surviving letters indicate that Hill placed his easel on the shore with the aim of painting 'the sea as a swamp', i.e. the lower shore at low tide, as well as the fluctuating patterns of sea and light.

7 **Axel Lindman (1848-1939)**
Apple Tree in Flower: Motif from Barbizon
Oil on panel, 16 x 27 cm.
Signed and dated 1877
Nationalmuseum NM 1786

Lindman trained in Paris from 1875 to 1879, after which he joined a colony of Swedish artists, including Elias Erdtman (cat. 9) who worked at Barbizon in the Forest of Fontainebleau during the following decades. There they developed the Realist ideas of the French painters who had settled in the village from the late 1840s, notably Jean-François Millet, Théodore Rousseau and Narcisse Diaz de la Peña. Essentially their aims were an exact and unidealised rendering of landscape scenery and peasant life, free from classical conventions and painted on the spot in a vibrant *non-finito* style. Much of their work was inspired by Dutch seventeenth-century landscapes and British artists, notably Constable and Bonington. Here Lindman takes an attractive feature isolated in bare farmland - a blossoming apple tree - as the central motif for his *plein-air* study. Similar subjects were painted by his French contemporaries, among them the Impressionist, Camille Pissarro.

8   **Axel Lindman (1848-1939)**
A Street in Fréjus
Oil on panel, 16 x 27 cm.
Signed and dated 1878
Nationalmuseum NM 1787

The strongly geometrical style of the background architecture, balanced foreground
motifs of trees and wall, together with the artist's tonal approach to colour, and
extensive use of the brown underpaint as part of the design, here suggest admiration
for the work of Corot. Lindman spent long periods in the late 1870s at Villerville on the
Normandy coast, but visited the small town of Fréjus in the southeast of France between
Cannes and Toulon in 1878, where he made this highly accomplished study. The brown
retaining wall to the right is likely to be part of the ancient town's extensive Roman ruins.
The work shares a quiet, intimate freshness with the many coastal scenes the artist
painted in France, Italy and Sweden.

9 Elias Erdtman (1862-1945)

The Laurent Boarding House, Grez-sur-Loing
Oil on canvas mounted on cardboard, 35 x 24 cm.
Signed and dated 1886
Nationalmuseum NM 3966

Erdtman moved to Grez in 1886, having studied in Düsseldorf and Paris. The village is about 70 kilometres south of Paris and ten from Fontainebleau. The Laurent Boarding House was one of the favourite *pensions* for his compatriots there and a rival of the better known Hôtel Chevillon. The village was described by visitors as simple and pleasant, not exactly beautiful, but picturesque. Corot had painted the bridge at Grez and several British and American artists worked there at the beginning of the 1880s. The first Swede to arrive was Hugo Salmson in the summer of 1874 but it was not until the following decade that Grez became a Swedish summer colony, comparable in size with Skagen in Denmark. This little picture was almost certainly painted on the spot. While Erdtman's structural handling of the architecture recalls the style of Corot, the deliberately imprecise handling of the grass and flowers in the foreground suggests the influence of the Realist, Jules Bastien-Lepage (1848-84).

10   **Bruno Liljefors (1860-1939)**
Jays
Oil on canvas, 51 x 66 cm.
Signed and dated 1886
Nationalmuseum NM 6811

Liljefors was a member of the 'Opponents' but alone in choosing the wildlife of his native Sweden as his main subject matter. From about 1880 he specialised in scenes of native birds, game and related subjects such as hunts, which led to his recognition as a 'national painter'. After a short period abroad, including visits to Düsseldorf, Paris and Grez, he settled in Kvarnbo, just outside Uppsala in central Sweden. His settings portray the creatures that he hunted there, within the often unremarkable habitat that had shaped their lives in the plains of Uppland. He frequently focuses on unidealised details of the landscape, such as the prominent foreground leaves here. In this characteristically asymmetrical composition, much of the background is less than clear, suggesting the hazier field of vision surrounding the pinpoint focus of the human eye. The two jays also seem caught in mid-movement, a device reminiscent of the arresting effect of photography. The artist was also affected by Japanese art, first evident during his visit to Paris and Grez in 1884 and apparent in the unconventional viewpoint of the present work - though he later was said to have denied oriental influence.

11 Karl Nordström (1855-1923)

View of Stockholm from Skansen

Oil on canvas, 62 x 121 cm.
Signed and dated 1889
Nationalmuseum NM 1891

Nordström arrived at Grez from Paris in the summer of 1882, having made his debut at the Salon and visited the seventh Impressionist exhibition; there he dedicated himself to a realistic, luminous *plein-air* style of painting. However, he did not lose contact with artistic life in Sweden but in 1885 co-founded the progressive Opponent movement *(Opponenterna)*, which included Liljefors (cat. 10) and Kreuger (cat. 15). On returning to his homeland the following year, he set up the Artists' Association *(Konstnärsförbundet)*, an exhibiting group to challenge the hegemony of the Stockholm Academy. In the present work, strongly reminiscent of Impressionist views of Paris from Montmartre, he shows the Swedish capital through haze from a vantage point near his home, emphasising the mundane landscape enveloping its historic centre. The view is from the hill of Skansen, on the island of Djurgården in northeast Stockholm, facing northwest across the Djurgårdsbrunnsviken. This picture may be seen as one of the most successful attempts to impose an Impressionist aesthetic on a Swedish subject, an approach that Nordström pioneered in the 1880s.

12 **August Strindberg (1849-1912)**
Little Water, Dalarö
Oil on cardboard, 22 x 33 cm.
1892
Nationalmuseum NM 6633

Renowned for his dramas and novels, Strindberg made his name in 1879 with *Röda Rummet* (*The Red Room*), a satirical novel about the art circles of Stockholm. Following his first divorce, he turned to art as a way of handling a personal and professional crisis and his paintings were mainly produced in periods of stress - in 1892-3, 1894 and the early 20th century. They reflect the existential turmoil of the artist's life in a highly original, proto-expressionist style, presaging his friendship with international modernists such as Gauguin and the Norwegian painter, Edvard Munch (1863-1944). *Little Water, Dalarö* exemplifies Strindberg's already unorthodox painting techniques, using thick impasto, passionately applied with a palette knife. Dalarö lies on the Baltic coast at the edge of the Stockholm archipelago and in a cottage there Strindberg painted about 30 seascapes over the summer of 1892. Featuring threatening waves, stormy seas, buoys and sea markers, and often seeming to anticipate abstraction, these were unsuccessfully exhibited at Stockholm.

13   Olof Arborelius (1842-1915)

Lake View at Engelsberg, Västmanland
Oil on canvas, 81 x 120 cm.
Signed and dated 1893
Nationalmuseum NM 1472

Västmanland is a region with numerous lakes about 60 miles to the northwest of Stockholm. The artist has captured both the vastness of this area and its rural isolation, emphasised by the empty boat in the foreground at the head of the motionless and seemingly limitless stretch of water. Nature seems barely touched by the presence of humankind yet despite the rocky shore, this is a friendly, summer landscape, open and brightly lit, though contemplated from the shadows. Such subjects had been developed as alternatives to the dramatic or dreamy visions of Romanticism. Arborelius was a pupil of Edvard Bergh (cat. 5) and, despite joining the Artists' Association, continued a conservative tradition of moderate Realism up to the turn of the century and beyond, retaining echoes of the Düsseldorf school and little affected by new developments. He spent every summer in a colony of artists at Engelsberg, an old iron working community in Bergslagen, central Sweden. This painting was taken to epitomise the concept of the Swedish national idyll as late as 1935, when it won a competition, organised by the Swedish Travel Association, to find the picture best representing the typically Swedish.

14 **Gustav Fjaestad (1868-1948)**
Winter Moonlight
Oil on canvas, 100 x 124 cm.
Signed and dated 1895
Nationalmuseum NM 1628

The silent, moonlit depths of the Swedish winter are hauntingly conveyed in a tradition pioneered in northern Europe by the German Romantic landscapist Caspar David Friedrich (1777-1840) and his Dresden circle, notably the Norwegian, Johan Christian Dahl. In Sweden winter themes had been rare but around the final decade of the 19th century they became a symbol of the search for a specific national character. Fjaestad, who had been an assistant to Liljefors (cat. 10), was a member of an artists' colony by Lake Racken in Värmland, west central Sweden. During the 1890s he worked in a Synthetist style, combining ornamental stylisation with an incisive realism. He developed a particular attachment to frozen lakes and wooded landscapes decked in snow and hoar frost. Although he often used photographs as a basis for his paintings, he played down illusionism, emphasising rather the unifying role of surface. Here a flat, pointillist pattern of dots and small patches of colour has been employed to create volume and visual excitement. This is strongly reinforced by the cropped image, a favourite device of the artist, who was influenced by Japanese woodblock prints.

15   Nils Kreuger (1858-1930)

The Håsten Hill at Varberg II
Oil on canvas, 77 x 117 cm.
Signed and dated 1896
Nationalmuseum NM 6823

Varberg was a spa and bathing resort in the province of Halland, south of Gothenburg on the southwest coast, which gave its name to the Varberg Group, an association of Kreuger, Richard Bergh (1858-1919) and Karl Nordström (cats. 11 & 29). They combined in the 1890s to pursue a *plein-air* style to depict inhospitable scenes, seeking to reflect the moods and atmosphere of the area by expressing the broad contours of the land in simplified forms. From 1893 Kreuger began to develop his own strongly distinctive pointillist idiom, using dots and short strokes laid over the paint. He had been impressed by Gauguin's work, exhibited in 1892 at Copenhagen, where *Landscape Brittany* was purchased by his friend Richard Bergh. There are also hints of Van Gogh about this picture, a number of whose drawings were shown in Copenhagen the following year at the Free Exhibition (*Den frie Udstillung*). These are particularly apparent in the sky and through the intensity of emotion conveyed by the desolate terrain. Kreuger executed more than one version of this subject, as indicated by the Roman numeral of the title.

16   **Eugène Jansson (1862-1915)**
Riddarfjärden, Stockholm
Oil on canvas, 150 x 135 cm.
Signed and dated 1898
Nationalmuseum NM 1699

Jansson was Sweden's supreme exponent of a subjective lyrical style of 'mood' painting and this work is one of the best examples of his dreamlike shimmering views of nocturnal Stockholm. Round the dark waters of Riddarfjärden, the glowing streetlights of the city mingle with reflections of the stars to form a decorative pattern, in which every outline has dissolved. From 1890 to 1905 Jansson's paintings lack any human figures, projecting an almost surreal sense of isolation, curiously at odds with the thronging life of the city, where he had a studio high above the central island of Södermalm. His blue paintings of this period, developed first in pastels and later in oils, eventually earned him the epithet 'the blue painter'. They emphasise space, atmosphere and light, couched in the fluid, expressive brushwork much in fashion at the time and reminiscent of the work of Van Gogh and Munch, the latter of whom first exhibited in Stockholm in 1894. Jansson is also likely also to have known Whistler's nocturnes - through reproductions, as he himself never left Sweden. His conjuring of atmospheric intensity and foreboding, however, remain uniquely his own and a major contribution to European landscape painting.

17   **Otto Hesselbom (1848-1913)**
Summer Night: Study
Oil on canvas, 55 x 92 cm.
Signed but undated
Nationalmuseum NM 4245

This is one of a number of studies which Hesselbom made in connection with his iconic painting *Our Country* (1902, Nationalmuseum), one of the best-known works of Swedish National Romanticism. The stylised panoramic view was based on his native province of Dalsland, in an area of central Sweden bordering Norway. Well known for its lakes, including part of the largest in the country, Lake Vänern, it was a region of dense forests and sparse population. Its seemingly boundless extent is viewed under the evocative conditions of a long summer twilight - a recurrent motif in Swedish art at the turn of the century. Contemplated through a lens of ineffable nostalgia and recast in Synthetist stylisation, this image was used by the artist in the larger work to create an intensely emotional silent space where quasi-religious yearnings could be subsumed in the monumental and timeless grandeur of Swedish nature.

18   **Prins Eugen (1865-1947)**
The Factory: View from Waldemarsudde towards the Old Saltsjökvarn
Oil on canvas, 90 x 100 cm.
Signed and dated 1906
Nationalmuseum NM 4239

Overall, Prins Eugen's paintings exemplify the Swedish interest in *plein-air* Realism. The youngest son of King Oscar II and nephew of Charles XV, he undertook several journeys to Italy in the 1880s and 1890s, his travelling companions including his friend and fellow artist, Richard Bergh. He was a pioneer of evocative Swedish landscape in the 1890s, with its National Romantic undercurrents, influenced especially by the Swiss painter, Arnold Böcklin, with twilight and night used as the main vehicles of emotion. In 1887 he spent some months in Paris as pupil at an art school, where the teachers included Puvis de Chavannes, and he first won acclaim as a painter in 1891. Uncharacteristically Prins Eugen's subject here is partly industrial, featuring the old Stockholm mill, viewed from Waldemarsudde, his residence across the Saltsjön on the island of Djurgården. In this respect the work relates to a notable genre of Swedish eighteenth-century painting, i.e. commissions from thriving iron masters, who had paintings made of their plants, often with their employees at work. Painted by such artists as Elias Martin and Pehr Hilleström (1732-1816), these were among the earliest industrial pictures in Europe.

Drawings and Watercolours

19   **Carl Johan Fahlcrantz (1774-1861)**
Sigtuna in Summer
Pencil, pen, black and grey wash, 27.2 x 37.2 cm.
Undated
Nationalmuseum NMH 410/1917

The founder of the Swedish school of landscape painting, Fahlcrantz studied at the Academy of Fine Arts in Stockholm. Rather than embarking on the customary study tour of Italy he decided to stay in Sweden and explore the natural scenery there. Yet he often worked in a highly Claudean style, presumably as a result of seeing prints after Claude, or works by his northern followers. Sigtuna is a small town 40 kilometres south of Uppsala with a historic past dating to Viking times. Founded in 980 by King Eric Segersäll, it grew from a village to become Sweden's foremost trading centre, supporting seven churches. Fahlcrantz focuses on the ruined tower of St Lars, one of the remaining ones, built in the 12th century. The rest of the town, already a subject of Romantic fascination, is seen behind and the entire scene is bathed in a lyrical glow of summer light. The instinctive classicism of Fahlcrantz was remarked upon by the architect, C.F. Sundvall in 1804: 'He has never seen anything else but this dreary country and yet he paints as if he had spent his whole life in Tivoli or Frascati.'

20 Gustav Wilhelm Palm (1810-1890)

Three Cypress Trees by a Fountain
Pencil, brown wash, brown chalk, heightened with white, 56.7 x 41.7 cm.
Signed, inscribed and dated 1842
Nationalmuseum NMH 1352/1924

Many Swedish artists travelled to Rome in the early 19th century, but relatively few chose to devote themselves to the depiction of classical landscape. Palm, however, became the foremost exponent of the classical tradition, and having spent the decade 1841-51 in Rome, committed the rest of his life to conventional studio paintings of an idealised world and large, finished studies. Here, however, he responds directly to a group of cypresses of a type so often encountered in Italy, which he recorded no doubt as part of his repertory for future use. The inscription records that the location is by the Baths of Diocletian, the largest imperial baths, in Rome. Palm continued to dress in a manner recalling his Italian days, with cape and broad-brimmed hat, for decades after his return to Sweden and was known as 'Palma Vecchio' to students of the Stockholm Academy. The Nationalmuseum holds about 1200 of his drawings and watercolours.

21 Gustav Wilhelm Palm (1810-1890)
View of Rome and the Tiber
Pencil and grey wash, heightened with white, 42.3 x 59.7 cm.
Signed, inscribed and dated 1846
Nationalmuseum NMH 339/1891

Like his first teacher, Fahlcrantz, Palm looked to Claude and Poussin as his main paradigms but was also much influenced by the ideas and forms of ideal landscape relayed through the large number of German artists in Rome, such as Johan Wilhelm Schirmer (1807-63), who later became the most influential landscape painter at Düsseldorf. During summer excursions round Rome, Palm made a great many oil studies, together with highly worked drawings like this one, on which his paintings were dependent after his return to Sweden. The inscription records the date of this drawing as 4 August 1846 and the location as 'Ripetta'. It is taken from the south of the city in Trastevere, looking northwards upriver towards the Porto di Ripa Grande, with Testaccio on the opposite bank, and in the distance the massive Ospizio di S. Michele. This area was an important harbour for goods brought to Rome by sea and thence by river from Ostia or Fiumicino. Further towards the viewer are the customs houses and the arsenal, while beyond S. Michele is a distant glimpse of the domed church of S. Andrea della Valle, and, to the left, the bell-tower of S. Maria in Trastevere.

22   **Marcus Larson (1825-1864)**
Waterfall in the Province of Småland
Pencil and charcoal, 30 x 35.4 cm.
Signed, about 1855
Nationalmuseum NMH 395/1937

Larson was inspired to move to Düsseldorf by the Nordic Art Exhibition, held in Stockholm in 1850. He arrived in 1852 and was deeply influenced by the German artist Andreas Achenbach's dramatic landscapes, which he developed so successfully as to become the most distinguished representative of the Düsseldorf school in Sweden. In 1855, now living in Paris, he produced one of the *tours de force* of Swedish wilderness painting, *Waterfall in Småland* (replica, Nationalmuseum). It was followed by a series of pictures set in this southern province, where broad rivers with mighty cataracts carve their way through rocky, forest-clad landscapes under stormy skies. In these Larson's theatrical handling of light and meticulous rendering of details lead to great immediacy and involvement of the spectator. They were achieved through painstaking studies from nature such as the present work, and an intimate, though rarely admitted, knowledge of photographs taken by his friend, C.G.W. Carleman. This drawing is closely related to the painting that caused such a sensation in Paris, where it served as a metaphor for the increasing Swedish sense of national identity.

23 August Malmström (1829-1901)

Study: Dancing Fairies
Pencil and watercolour, 15.9 x 28 cm.
1866
Nationalmuseum NMH 125/1902

The isolated countryside and regional idiosyncrasies gave rise to much traditional Swedish folklore. In this small yet vivacious study Malmström imagines an ethereal troop of fairies or elves dancing in remote woodland by the light of the moon. In 1866 he worked the subject up into a large painting entitled *Dance of the Elves*, which was acquired by the King and left to the Nationalmuseum. This reflected the more fanciful side of his lifelong interest in Scandinavian culture. In the mid-19th century, such subjects were the very essence of northern European Romanticism, extending from Scandinavia through Germany to England.

24   **Carl Fredrik Hill (1849-1911)**
Landscape with Trees
Charcoal and white chalk on grey paper, 40.5 x 41 cm.
Signed and dated 1876
Nationalmuseum NMH 23/1917

After a short period at the Academy of Fine Arts in Stockholm, Hill was one of a number of Swedish painters who followed Wahlberg (cat. 4) in turning to Paris as the source for new artistic developments. He went on to produce particularly expressive landscapes during the 1870s and was the first Swedish artist to speak of the Impressionists in positive terms. In 1876 he visited Manet's studio and, seeing the works that had been refused by the Salon, described them as 'the most realistic current of art at present'. Unsurprisingly, all but one of Hill's own works were rejected by the jury of the Paris Salon, although the dealer Durand-Ruel showed those refused for the Salon of 1876 and Hill was invited to exhibit with the Impressionists at their second exhibition, held that year. The same autumn he went to Luc-sur-Mer in Normandy, where this beautifully composed study of trees may have been executed (see also cat. 6).

25 **Carl Fredrik Hill (1849-1911)**
Ravens on a Snow-covered Plain
Black, white and coloured chalk, 17.2 x 21 cm.
Undated
Nationalmuseum NMH 178/1926

Hill enjoyed a few years of intensive and brilliantly original painting in France before 1878, when he succumbed to mental illness. In January that year he was admitted to an asylum at Passy and returned to Sweden in about 1880 to his native town of Lund, remaining there until his death three decades later. In spring 1883 he was transferred from a psychiatric hospital to his family home, to live with his mother and sister, Hedda. There with great intensity he worked on thousands of drawings, many of a highly charged or disturbed appearance as in the present case, a fantasy of predatory-looking ravens - birds with potent significance in Viking and Norse mythology - in an empty landscape. For the most part he used crayons and black chalk but he also filled large sheets of paper with compositions in ink and gold and silver paint.

26 Edvard Bergh (1828-1880)

Forest Lake
Pencil, 20.9 x 29.1 cm.
Undated
Nationalmuseum NMH 37/1892

Edvard Bergh has been described as the portrayer *par excellence* of the central Swedish landscape. He was a pupil of Hans Gude at Düsseldorf, and led the landscape school established in 1858 at the Stockholm Academy. Many of his paintings are dominated by a placid river and sunlit birches, often with a cowherd and cattle in the foreground (cat. 5). Here, however, the artist responds directly to the scene before his eyes, arranging the water, trees and rocks in a subtle way so as to lead the viewer's attention gently into the composition. The varying intensity of the light among the trees and the mirror-like surface of the lake contribute to the peaceful, idyllic mood of the prospect. A contemporary critic once noted the softness of the outlines of Bergh's trees against surrounding air - an effect that has already been captured in this drawing.

27 **Anders Zorn (1860-1920)**
Study of Landscape from Mora
Watercolour, 30.3 x 18.9 cm.
Signed and dated 1886
Nationalmuseum NMH 116/1987

Zorn was among those Swedish painters who after 1870 turned to France for inspiration. During the 1880s he travelled widely, visiting London, Paris, Spain, Algiers and even Istanbul, and developing a virtuoso watercolour technique. He found much inspiration in Impressionism, particularly after about 1888, when he turned to oil and moved to Paris. There he knew the intellectual circles that included the journalist, politician and former minister of arts, Antonin Proust (1832-1905). Regarding the countryside as his true subject matter, however, he returned to Sweden in 1896 and settled permanently in rural seclusion in his native Mora at the northwestern tip of Lake Siljan in the province of Dalarna. His swift, elegant and colourful Impressionist technique was given full rein in spontaneous views and studies of his surroundings there, such as the present early work. Conventionally hailed as Sweden's most famous painter, Zorn also produced etchings justly regarded as among the finest examples of Swedish graphic art. Internationally, he is perhaps best known, however, as a figurative artist - not least on account of his pictures of peasant girls bathing and portraits of American luminaries.

28 **Nils Kreuger (1858-1930)**
Landscape with Geese
Pencil, pen and black ink, coloured chalk, 27.5 x 48 cm.
Signed and dated 1893
Nationalmuseum NMH 16/1945

During the 1890s Kreuger converted the essential Swedish landscapes of forests and lakes, and the long twilights of the Scandinavian summer, into consummate works characterised by a blurring of spatial boundaries and a neglect of the rules of perspective, as evident in this drawing. Between 1893 and 1895, he lived at Varberg (cf. cat. 15) along with Richard Bergh and Karl Nordström (cat. 29) but even before then he had begun to abandon the Realist style favoured by all three artists in the 1880s. Together they embarked on a Synthetist manner, using dark outlines and large, unbroken areas of colour that emphasised the basic mood of a landscape rather than reproducing its details. Significant factors in this development were their knowledge of Gauguin and Van Gogh, both of whose expressive graphic idioms are used here. Kreuger's search for the artistic style most suited to the natural landscape of Halland allowed him to accentuate the forms of the terrain and achieve great emotional depth. In this case, though, the line of geese adds a reassuringly domestic touch to the otherwise desolate scene.

29 **Karl Nordström (1855-1923)**
The Schoolhouse at Varberg
Black chalk, 60.2 x 47.8 cm.
Undated; 1893-96
Nationalmuseum NMH 182/1957

A former Realist, Nordström was quick to search for new ideals. After a year at the Stockholm Academy he went to Paris in 1880, where he studied contemporary art, and then spent a period at Grez, developing a luminous, *plein-air* style that he retained into the 1890s. From then on the influence of Japanese prints and Gauguin became paramount. He left Stockholm in 1892 for the barren west-coast landscape of his home territory on the island of Tjörn commenting that 'we seem to need the wilderness to maintain our health and strength'. The following spring he moved with his family to Varberg, where his friend, Nils Kreuger, was already living (cat. 28). There they were joined in the autumn by Richard Bergh, son of Edvard, forming the 'Varberg Group'. In his search for the isolated, peaceful and primitive Nordström may be seen as a kindred spirit to Gauguin and in character, too there were parallels, as noted by Bergh in 1893, when he described his colleague as a 'painting, roaring lion'. Stylistically Nordström moved towards Gauguin's Synthetist approach but remained more emotive, as in this drawing, where the schoolhouse, silhouetted against a frenzied sky, is endowed with monumental form and brooding significance.

Select English Bibliography

Dreams of a Summer Night: Scandinavian Painting at the Turn of the Century, exh. cat., Hayward Gallery, London, 1986.

Eugène Jansson, exh. cat., Liljevalchs Konsthall, Stockholm, 1998 [summary in English].

Facos, Michelle, *Nationalism and the Nordic Imagination: Swedish Art of the 1890s*, Berkeley, Los Angeles and London, 1998.

Granath, Olle, *August Strindberg, Painter, Photographer, Writer*, exh. cat., Tate Modern, 2005.

Gunnarsson, Torsten, *Nordic Landscape Painting in the Nineteenth Century*, translated by Nancy Adler, New Haven and London, 1998.

In the Realm of the Wild: The Art of Bruno Liljefors in Sweden, exh. cat., Gothenburg, New York, Minnesota, 1988.

Kent, Neil, *The Triumph of Light and Nature in Nordic Art, 1740-1940*, London, 1987.

Nasgaard, Roald, *The Mystic North: Symbolist Landscape Painting in Northern Europe and North America, 1890-1940*, exh. cat., Art Gallery of Ontario, Toronto, 1984.

Polfeldt, Ingegerd, *Möte med Carl Fredrik Hill* [Carl Fredrik Hill - An Introduction], Mälmö Museum, Mälmö, 1980 [summary in English].

Rosenblum, Robert, *The Paintings of August Strindberg: The Structure of Chaos*, Bløndal, Hellerup, 1995.

Sandström, Birgitta, *Anders Zorn, 1860-1920: An Introduction to his Life and Achievements*, Zorn Collections, Mora, 1996.

The Painter of Swedish Life, Carl Larsson, exh. cat., Tokyo, Kumamoto, Mie, Niigata, 1994.

Usselman, Henri, *Complexité et importance des contacts des peintres Nordiques avec l'impressionisme*, Gothenburg, 1979 [summary in English].

Varnedoe, Kirk, *Northern Light: Realism and Symbolism in Scandinavian Painting, 1880-1910*, exh. cat., Washington D.C., New York and Minneapolis, 1982.